59372083604259   MOSQ

WITHDRAWN

D0828506

My Path to Math

Regrouping

Claire Piddock

Crabtree Publishing Company

www.crabtreebooks.com

Author: Claire Piddock
Publishing plan research and development:
  Sean Charlebois, Reagan Miller
  Crabtree Publishing Company
Editor: Reagan Miller
Proofreader: Crystal Sikkens
Editorial director: Kathy Middleton
Project coordinator: Margaret Salter
Prepress technician: Margaret Salter
Series editor: Jessica Cohn
Coordinating editor: Chester Fisher
Project manager: Kumar Kunal (Q2AMEDIA)
Art direction: Cheena Yadav (Q2AMEDIA)
Cover design: Isha Khanna (Q2AMEDIA)
Design: Suzena Samuel (Q2AMEDIA)
Photo research: Nivisha Sinha (Q2AMEDIA)
3D Illustartions: Gopal Das

Photographs:
Istockphoto: William Howell: p. 7, 15; Richard Gunion: p. 21
Dreamstime: Flamingpumpkin: p. 12 (top), p. 19;
  Jillekulchinsky: p. 18 (bottom)
Q2AMedia Art Bank : 15, 16, 17, 19, 20, 23.
Other images by Shutterstock

Library and Archives Canada Cataloguing in Publication

Piddock, Claire
        Regrouping / Claire Piddock.

(My path to math)
Includes index.
ISBN 978-0-7787-6785-5 (bound).--ISBN 978-0-7787-6794-7 (pbk.)

        1. Addition--Juvenile literature. 2. Subtraction--Juvenile literature.
I. Title. II. Series: My path to math

QA115.P516 2010   j513.2'11   C2010-901013-2

Library of Congress Cataloging-in-Publication Data

Piddock, Claire.
  Regrouping / Claire Piddock.
    p. cm. -- (My path to math)
  Includes index.
  ISBN 978-0-7787-6785-5 (reinforced lib. bdg. : alk. paper) -- ISBN 978-0-7787-6794-7 (pbk. : alk. paper)
  1. Addition--Juvenile literature. 2. Subtraction--Juvenile literature. 3. Group theory--Juvenile literature. I. Title. II. Series.

QA115.P58 2011
513.2'11--dc22

2010004528

Crabtree Publishing Company

www.crabtreebooks.com   1-800-387-7650

Printed in China/082010/AP20100512

Published in Canada
Crabtree Publishing
616 Welland Ave.
St. Catharines, ON
L2M 5V6

Published in the United States
Crabtree Publishing
PMB 59051
350 Fifth Avenue, 59th Floor
New York, New York 10118

Published in the United Kingdom
Crabtree Publishing
Maritime House
Basin Road North, Hove
BN41 1WR

Published in Australia
Crabtree Publishing
386 Mt. Alexander Rd.
Ascot Vale (Melbourne)
VIC 3032

Contents

Downtown Diner

On Saturday, Betsy helps Aunt Essie at her diner. Betsy's first job is to gather the straws. She finds one group of ten straws.

Next to that are three single straws. That is 13 straws in all. The number 13 is 1 group of ten and 3 ones.

Next, Betsy finds four more single straws. She now has 17 straws.

13 + 4 = 17

The number 17 is the **sum**. A sum is the answer to an addition problem.

Activity Box

Now, try adding 23 and 4. Start at 23, which is 2 groups of ten and 3 ones. Count four places to the right on the **number line**.

0 1 2 3 4 5 6 7 8 9 10 11 12 13 14 15 16 17 18 19 20 21 22 23 24 25 26 27 28 29 30

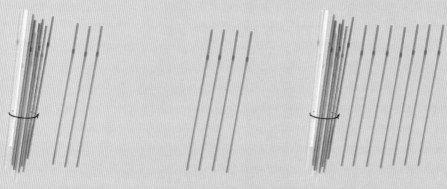

1 ten 3 ones   +   4 ones   =   1 ten 7 ones

You can check Betsy's sum on a number line. Start at 13 and count four places to the right.

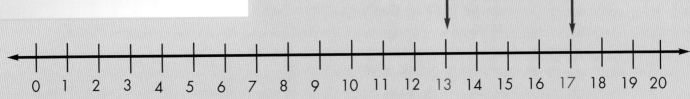

13 + 4 = 17

Adding Without Regrouping

Betsy has 17 straws so far. Then she finds 11 more straws on a table. How many does she have in all?

17 + 11 = ?

Betsy uses a pencil and paper to find the total. First, she lines up the **digits** in a **place-value chart**. Next, she writes out an addition problem for 17 plus 11. She adds the numbers in the ones column first. After that, she adds the numbers in the tens column. Betsy has 28 straws.

tens	ones
1	7
1	1

17
+ 11
‾‾‾‾

Activity Box

Add the straws below. Use a place-value chart to help you line up the numbers.

tens	ones

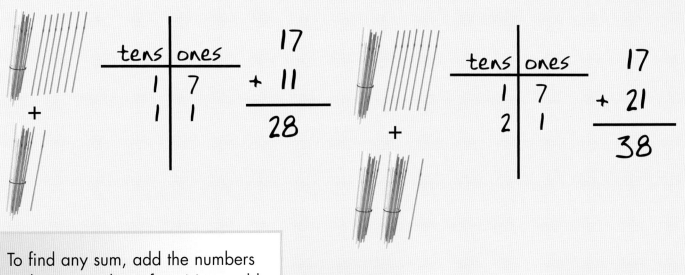

$$\begin{array}{c|c} \text{tens} & \text{ones} \\ \hline 1 & 7 \\ 1 & 1 \end{array}$$

$$\begin{array}{r} 17 \\ + 11 \\ \hline 28 \end{array}$$

$$\begin{array}{c|c} \text{tens} & \text{ones} \\ \hline 1 & 7 \\ 2 & 1 \end{array}$$

$$\begin{array}{r} 17 \\ + 21 \\ \hline 38 \end{array}$$

To find any sum, add the numbers in the ones column first. Next, add the numbers in the tens column.

Regrouping in Addition

To count the straws, Betsy thinks about groups of ten.

Look to the right. Count ⟶ the groups of ten and then the ones.

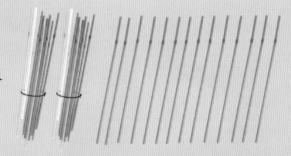

There are 2 groups of ten and 14 ones. That is a lot of single straws to count. To make it easier, you can use **regrouping** instead. You can group 10 of the ones together to make another group of ten.

The 2 tens and 14 ones are the same as 3 tens and 4 ones. There are 34 straws in total.

Activity Box

Use beans or pennies to make a group of ten and a big pile of ones. Then see how many tens are in the pile. Regroup to find the total.

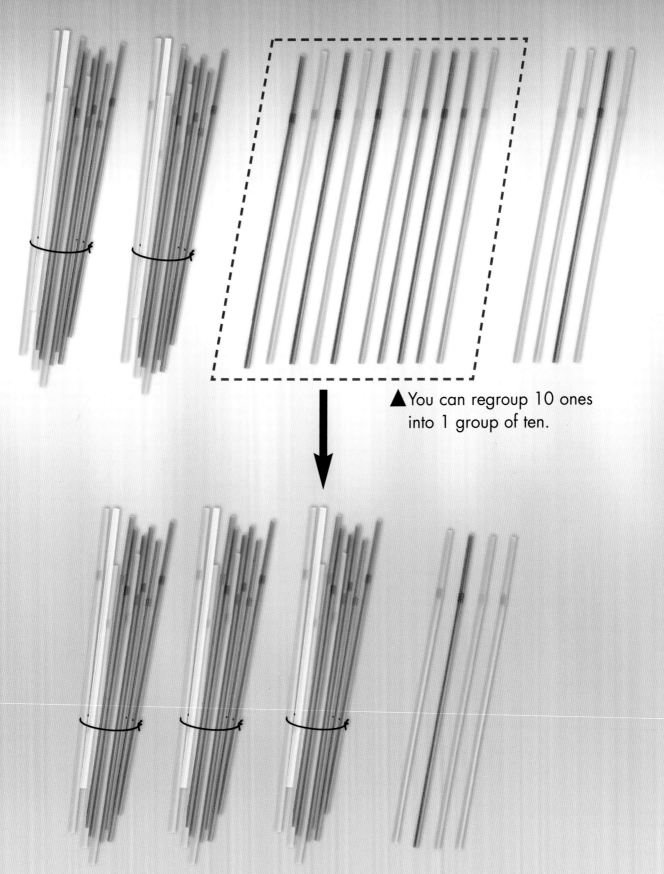

▲You can regroup 10 ones into 1 group of ten.

The 2 tens and 14 ones are the same as 3 tens and 4 ones.

Time to Add

Between jobs, Betsy does homework at the diner. In the morning, she works on homework for 27 minutes. In the afternoon, she does homework for 16 minutes.

How many minutes does she spend on homework altogether?

Betsy writes out a math problem for 27 plus 16. Look on page 11 to see how Betsy solves the math problem.

She starts by adding the numbers in the ones column. She adds 7 plus 6 and gets 13. She cannot write 13 in the ones column! She needs to regroup 10 ones as 1 ten. She can write a 1 at the top of the tens column to show the regrouping. Then she can add the tens.

Activity Box

How many minutes does it take you to get dressed in the morning? How many minutes does it take you to eat breakfast? Add the number of minutes together to find the total time it takes you to get dressed and eat breakfast.

Add the numbers in the ones column. Regroup if needed. You can write 1 in the tens column to show regrouping. Next, add the numbers in the tens column.

You can show regrouping this way.

1
27
+ 16
43

tens	ones
2	7
1	6

27
+ 16

Adding Money

Aunt Essie shows Betsy a bill for two meals. One meal costs $18. The other meal costs $17.

Betsy finds the total. First, she adds the numbers in the ones column. She adds 8 plus 7 and gets 15. She writes 5 below the ones column. Then she regroups 10 ones into 1 ten. She puts the 1 at the top of the tens column. Next, she adds the three numbers in the tens column. She adds 1 plus 1 plus 1. You can see her work on the top of the next page.

Downtown Diner

SERVER	TABLE	GUESTS	CHECK NUMBER
			926962

Pasta Dinner $18

Fish and Chips $17

TAX

TOTAL

Activity Box

Betsy has saved $28 at home. Aunt Essie will give her $8 for helping out. How much will Betsy have then?

$$\begin{array}{r} \$\ 28 \\ +\ \$\ 8 \\ \hline \end{array}$$

$$\begin{array}{r} \overset{1}{}\$18 \\ +\$17 \\ \hline \$35 \end{array}$$

Regrouping helps when adding money, too.

Subtraction

Aunt Essie asks Betsy to put one saltshaker at each table. There are eight tables.

Betsy finds 19 saltshakers on a shelf. She takes away eight of them. How many are left?

Look at the next page. Each block stands for one saltshaker. The place-value chart shows how to line up the digits for 19 minus 8.

Now, look at the math problem. Subtract the numbers in the ones column first. Then subtract the numbers in the tens column. The answer to a subtraction problem is called the **difference**.

There are 11 saltshakers left. You can check the difference on the number line.

Activity Box

Look at this number line. Now, write out a subtraction problem that shows the same thing.

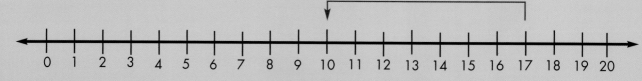

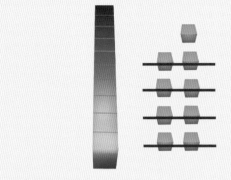

tens	ones
1	9
	8

$$\begin{array}{r} 19 \\ -\ 8 \\ \hline 11 \end{array}$$

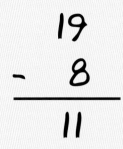

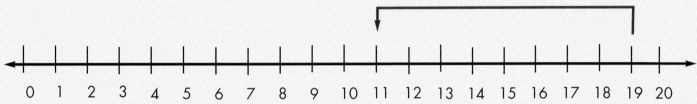

0 1 2 3 4 5 6 7 8 9 10 11 12 13 14 15 16 17 18 19 20

Begin at 19. Count eight places to the left.

Regrouping in Subtraction

Aunt Essie starts the day with 25 bagels. Some of the girls from Betsy's basketball team stop by. They order eight bagels. How many bagels are left?

Look at the top of the next page. Each block stands for one bagel. The blocks show how 25 can be regrouped. The place-value chart shows how to line up digits for the problem. To find the answer, start with the ones column. You cannot subtract 8 from 5. Regroup 1 ten into 10 ones, and change 5 to 15 in the ones column. Then subtract 8 from 15. Next, subtract the remaining tens.

Activity Box

Subtract 33 from 51. When there are not enough ones to subtract, regroup 1 ten into 10 ones.

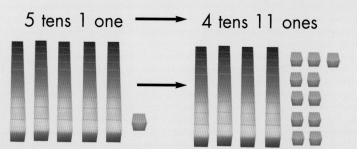

5 tens 1 one ⟶ 4 tens 11 ones

tens	ones
5	1
3	3

$$\begin{array}{r} \overset{4}{5}\overset{11}{1} \\ -\ 33 \\ \hline \end{array}$$

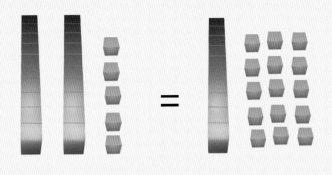

2 tens   5 ones   1 ten   15 ones

tens	ones
2	5
	8

$$\begin{array}{r} {\scriptstyle 1\ 15} \\ \cancel{25} \\ -\ \ 8 \\ \hline 17 \end{array}$$

What is 25 bagels minus 8 bagels?
Use regrouping to find the answer.

Time to Subtract

One customer has a bill for $14. He gives Betsy a twenty-dollar bill.

Betsy says, "I can find the **change**!" She writes down the math problem for 20 dollars minus 14 dollars.

Uh-oh! She cannot subtract 4 from 0.

Betsy thinks about the problem. She figures out what to do. She needs to regroup 1 ten and move it to the ones column.

The man gets $6 change.

Activity Box

You have 76 cents. You spend 20 cents. How much money do you have left? Do you need to regroup? Explain.

$20
-$14

2 tens

1 tens 10 ones

tens	ones
2	0
1	4

1 10
$2̶0̶
-$14
_____
$ 6

What is $20 minus $14?
Regroup the numbers to
find the answer.

Downtown Diner

SERVER

TABLE

GUESTS

CHECK NUMBER
926962

Greek Chicken Salad $14

TAX

TOTAL

Add and Subtract

At closing time, Betsy's dad comes to pick her up. Betsy has helped Aunt Essie at the diner. Aunt Essie has helped Betsy, too!

Betsy has learned about regrouping.

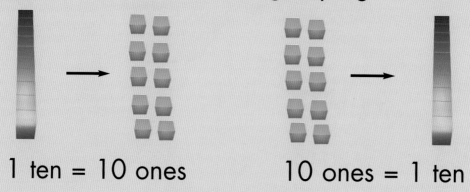

1 ten = 10 ones   10 ones = 1 ten

Sometimes you need to group 10 ones into 1 ten, so you can add. Sometimes you need to break apart 1 ten into 10 ones, so you can subtract.

Betsy has learned how to find sums and differences with regrouping!

Activity Box

Think of times when you need to add or subtract. Do you need to regroup to find the sum? Do you need to regroup to find the difference?

When the diner opens
again, there will be
more regrouping to do!

addition: no regrouping needed	addition: regrouping needed	subtraction: no regrouping needed	subtraction: regrouping needed
45 + 13 — 58	1 45 + 29 — 74	66 - 52 — 14	5 16 6̶6̶ - 18 — 48

Glossary

change The money left over or returned after a sum is paid

difference Answer to a subtraction problem

digits The symbols 0, 1, 2, 3, 4, 5, 6, 7, 8, and 9

number line Line with equally spaced tick marks named by numbers

place value Value assigned to each digit in a number based on its location in the number

place-value chart A chart that has columns for each place value

regrouping Exchanging amounts of equal value to rename a number; example: 2 tens 8 ones = 1 ten 18 ones

sum Answer to an addition problem

tens	ones
4	0
2	7

$$
\begin{array}{r}
\overset{3}{}\ \overset{10}{} \\
\$\,\cancel{40} \\
-\ \$\,27 \\
\hline
\$\,13
\end{array}
$$

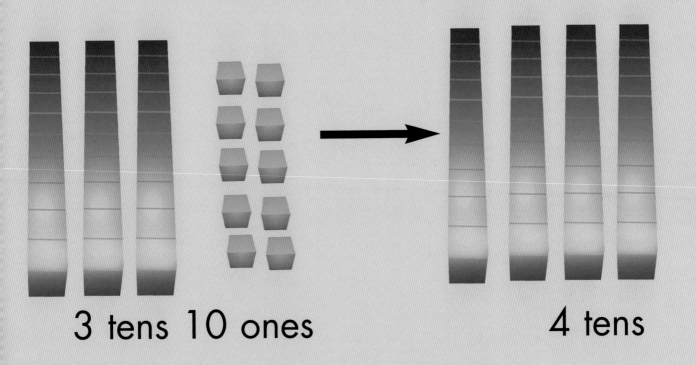

3 tens 10 ones   4 tens

Index